Taking EARTH'S Temperature

Climate Scientists at Work

Rebecca E. Hirsch

Rourke Educational Media
rourkeeducationalmedia.com

Before & After Reading Activities

Before Reading:

Building Academic Vocabulary and Background Knowledge

Before reading a book, it is important to tap into what your child or students already know about the topic. This will help them develop their vocabulary, increase their reading comprehension, and make connections across the curriculum.

1. *Look at the cover of the book. What will this book be about?*
2. *What do you already know about the topic?*
3. *Let's study the Table of Contents. What will you learn about in the book's chapters?*
4. *What would you like to learn about this topic? Do you think you might learn about it from this book? Why or why not?*
5. *Use a reading journal to write about your knowledge of this topic. Record what you already know about the topic and what you hope to learn about the topic.*
6. *Read the book.*
7. *In your reading journal, record what you learned about the topic and your response to the book.*
8. *After reading the book complete the activities below.*

Content Area Vocabulary

Read the list. What do these words mean?

absorb
atmosphere
glaciers
microscopic
migrate
observatory
particles
sediment
simulate
transmitted

After Reading:

Comprehension and Extension Activity

After reading the book, work on the following questions with your child or students in order to check their level of reading comprehension and content mastery.

1. *What can ice cores tell us about past climates? (Summarize)*
2. *How could you learn what the climate was like two hundred years ago in your city or town? (Infer)*
3. *What can satellites reveal about the Greenland ice sheet? (Asking Questions)*
4. *What animals might be affected by shifting seasons where you live? (Text to Self Connection)*
5. *How do scientists test whether their climate models are accurate? (Asking Questions)*

Extension Activity

Pick a wild animal in your area and research its habitat. Does it stay in your area all year long or does it migrate? If it migrates, where does it go? How is this animal being affected by climate change? Draw a diagram of the animal and a map of where it lives. Include information about how it could be affected by climate change.

TABLE OF CONTENTS

CHAPTER ONE

EARTH'S CHANGING CLIMATE

Climate is the normal weather in a city or region over a long period of time. The climate in Phoenix, Arizona, is hot and dry, while the climate in Antarctica is very cold. Earth's climate is the average of all the regional climates around the world.

Arizona has a hot climate year-round, while Antarctica's climate is very cold.

Climate can change over time. The average summer temperature for a city could rise, for example. Or the average annual snowfall for a region could fall. The climate of the planet can change too.

An area of cold air meeting an area of warm air brings in a storm.

CLIMATE VS. WEATHER

Weather refers to short-term conditions, such as if it is rainy or sunny outside. Weather can change quickly. The morning weather may be dry, while the afternoon can bring a thunderstorm. Climate can change too, but it doesn't change quickly the way weather does.

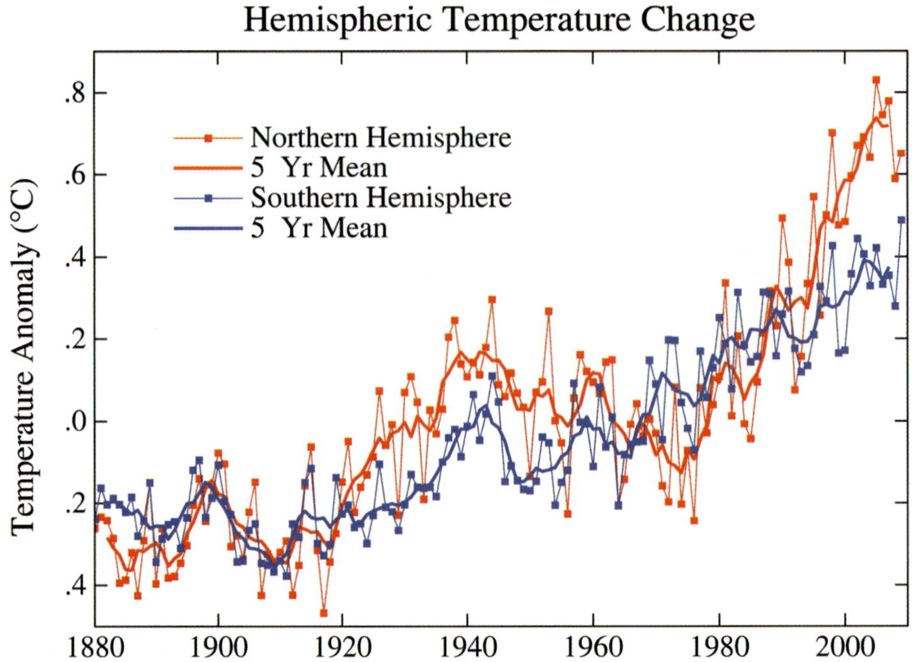

Most climate scientists agree that Earth's climate is growing warmer. They tell us that Earth's average temperature has risen by about 1.4 degrees Fahrenheit (0.8 degrees Celsius) over the last hundred years.

FROZEN PLANET

Earth's climate has changed many times in the past. Over the last million years, huge ice sheets have spread over the Earth and shrunk back several times.

Climate can change from natural events. Earth's climate can change from a large volcanic eruption, for instance, or from slight changes in the amount of energy from the sun.

Gases released from a volcanic eruption can change the climate.

But most climate scientists agree that the current warming can not be explained by natural events alone. Most of the warming of the last hundred years is very likely caused by the burning of fossil fuels.

When fossil fuels, such as oil and coal, are burned, carbon dioxide goes into the air. Carbon dioxide is a greenhouse gas. That means it traps heat from the sun and prevents the heat from escaping into space.

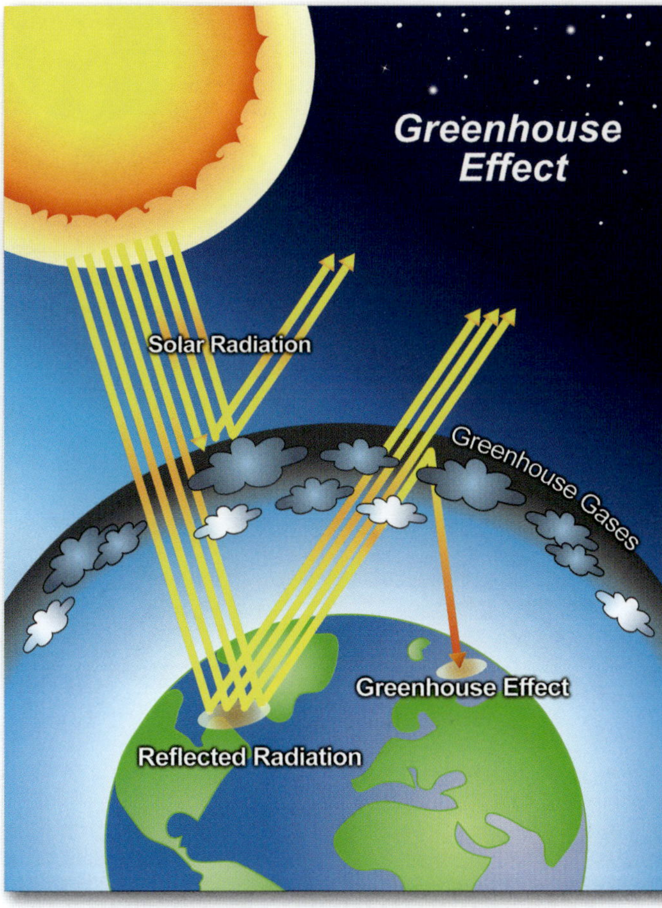

John Tyndall
1820 – 1893

EARTH'S THERMOSTAT

In the 1850s, Irish scientist John Tyndall discovered that nitrogen and oxygen in the ***atmosphere*** *allow light and heat to pass freely. Other gases, like carbon dioxide and water vapor, trap heat from the sun. Tyndall realized that heat-trapping gases help set Earth's temperature.*

Scientists around the world are working to understand our changing climate. They want to study what is happening to the climate now, investigate how the climate has changed in the past, and try to predict how it will change in the future.

Scientists take samples from sea ice in Antarctica.

CHAPTER TWO

TAKING THE PLANET'S TEMPERATURE

When scientists measure Earth's temperature, they do not take just one temperature reading. There is not a single temperature for the planet. They measure the Earth's weather every day at weather stations all around the world.

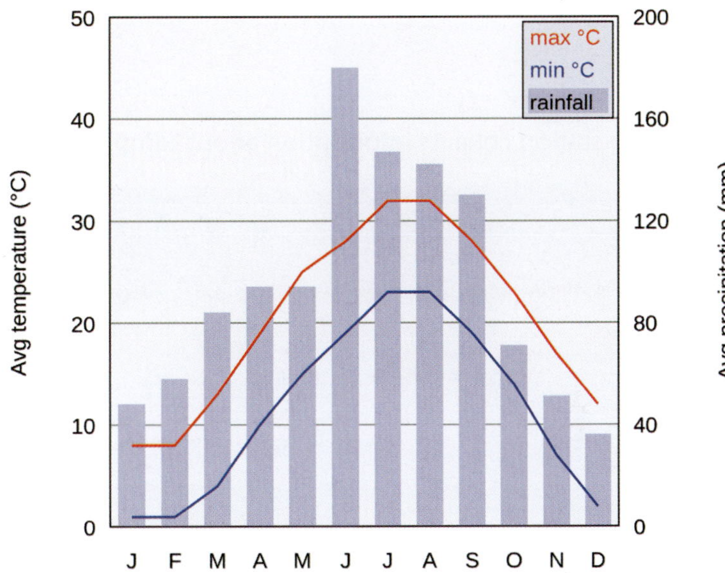

A scientist measures the activity of the sun.

ACTIVITY

MORNING, NOON, NIGHT

How does temperature change throughout the day? Record the temperature every two or three hours for several days. What is the hottest part of the day? What is the coldest? After several days, how closely can you predict the mid-afternoon temperature based on the noon temperature?

Thousands of weather stations measure the weather on land and at sea. They measure the weather at the frozen poles, in tropical jungles, and in deserts. These stations measure temperature, rainfall, humidity, and many other conditions. Satellites also measure the temperature of the Earth's surface.

A weather station collects information about temperature, humidity, and air pressure in Florida.

Sailing drones help gather information from remote parts of the oceans. These 19-foot (5.8-meter) long sailboats are powered by wind. Solar panels run the instruments. These drones can collect two million measurements per day, and transmit them via satellites. That way scientists can study climate and ocean conditions as they happen.

Sailing drones give researchers a way to monitor the oceans remotely.

Global Temperature

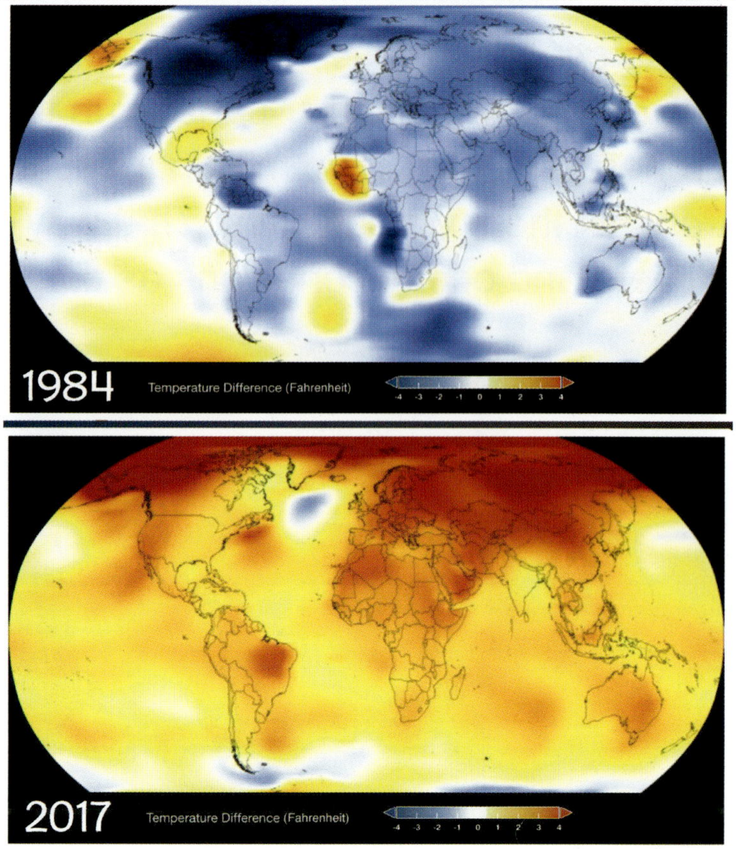

Scientists study many different readings to get snapshots of the Earth's climate. Scientists can create an average of these readings to learn how conditions at the Earth's surface are changing.

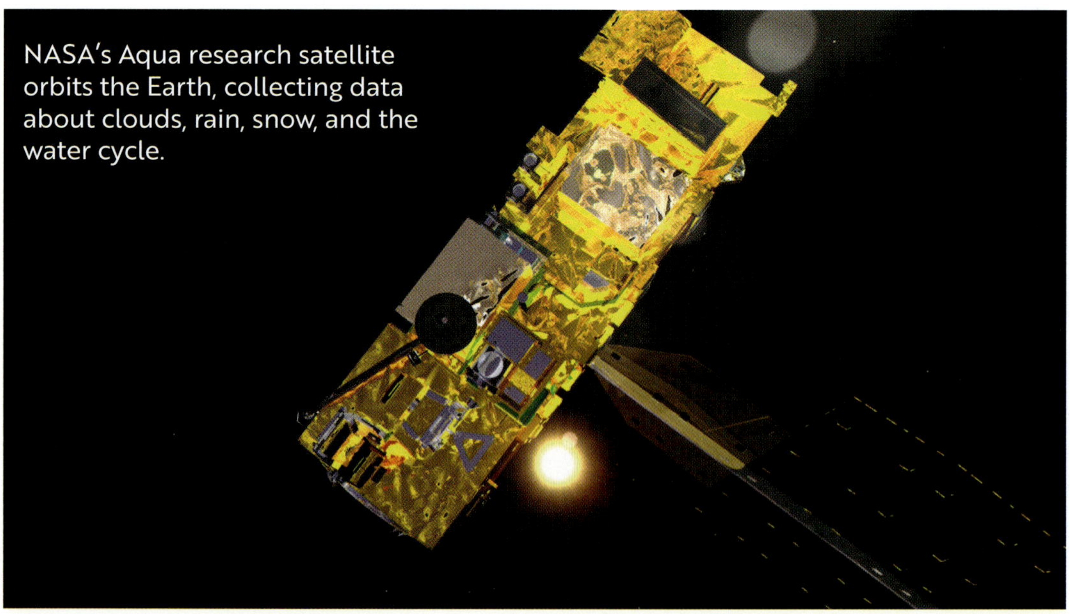

NASA's Aqua research satellite orbits the Earth, collecting data about clouds, rain, snow, and the water cycle.

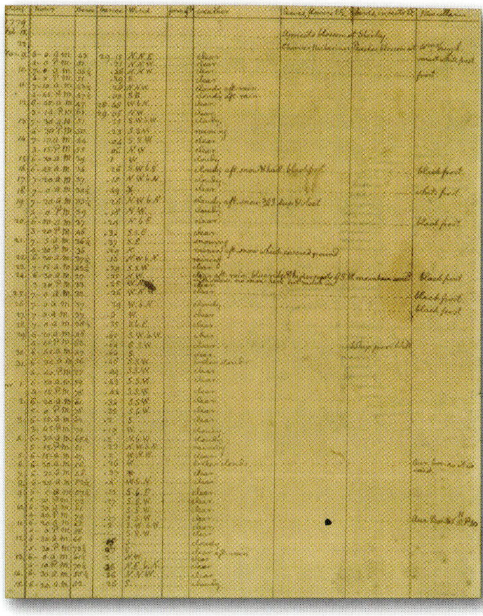

Weather records, like those kept by Thomas Jefferson, help us understand how weather has changed.

People have kept careful weather measurements for only about a hundred years. If scientists wish to learn what the weather was like a few hundred years ago, they can turn to weather journals. Careful observers such as Thomas Jefferson kept detailed weather journals. These records can give a glimpse of weather conditions of the recent past.

In 1881, Adolphus Greely led a 25-person expedition to establish a weather station in the Arctic.

Adolphus Washington Greely
1844-1935

Thomas Jefferson
1743 – 1826

WEATHER MAN

Thomas Jefferson kept detailed logs of the weather for many years. He recorded precipitation, temperature range, and cloud cover wherever he was—at home in Virginia or while traveling. He established a small network of weather observers in Virginia. The National Weather Service calls him the "father of weather observers."

Scientists can also measure carbon dioxide in the atmosphere to understand how it is changing. Since the 1950s, a weather **observatory** in Hawaii has measured how much carbon dioxide is in the atmosphere. This record, along with other measurements around the globe, reveal that carbon dioxide in the atmosphere is rising.

Since 1958, scientists have been measuring rising carbon dioxide at the Mauna Loa Observatory.

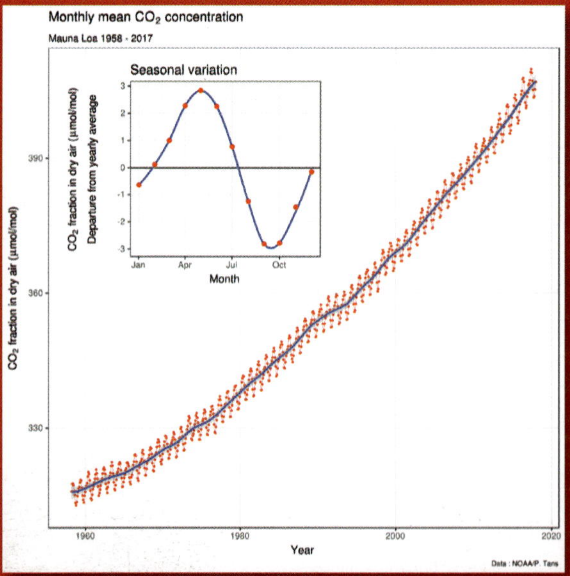

JAGGED CURVE

Carbon dioxide in the atmosphere falls in summer and rises in winter. The reason is that plants in the Northern Hemisphere ***absorb*** *carbon dioxide for growth in summer, but not in winter. The yearly measurement of carbon dioxide looks like the edge of a saw, with a tooth for each year.*

CHAPTER THREE

MEASURING THE MELT

As the climate warms, Earth's ice is melting. This ice sits on mountaintops, floats on cold ocean waters, and makes up **glaciers** and ice sheets near the poles.

As the climate grows warmer, Greenland's glaciers are shrinking.

The melting of ice sheets is very important. These huge sheets of ice cover Greenland and Antarctica. They contain enormous amounts of water. When the ice melts, the water runs off into the oceans and can cause sea levels to rise.

A vast ice sheet covers roughly 80 percent of the surface of Greenland.

SHEETS OF ICE

Ice sheets form when snow falls each year but does not melt completely. Over thousands of years, the layers of snow pile up. They become squeezed by their own weight and turn to ice.

BIG FOOTPRINT

The ice sheet in Antarctica would cover the contiguous United States and Mexico. The ice sheet in Greenland is three times the size of Texas. Together these ice sheets contain 99 percent of all freshwater on Earth.

Where Antarctica's ice sheet meets the sea, giant icebergs are breaking off.

Understanding the melting of the ice sheets is a big challenge for climate scientists. They want to understand how much and how fast the ice is melting. They also hope to learn how much of the melting is natural and how much is caused by the activities of people.

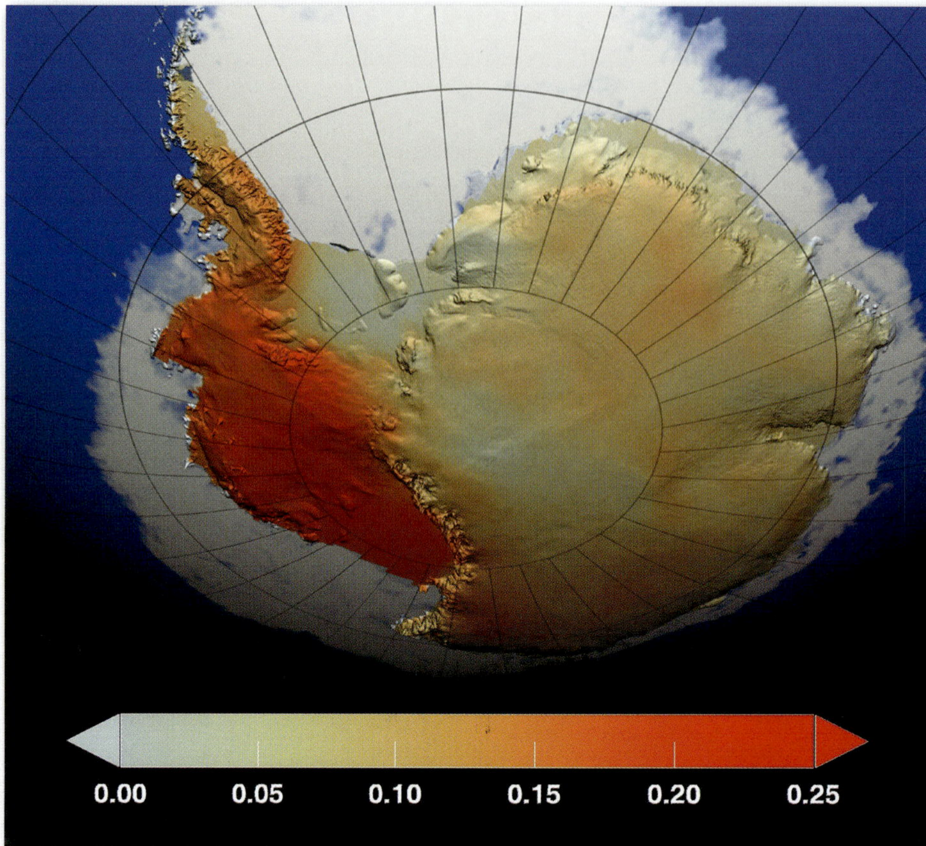

Fifty years of temperature measurements show that Antarctica is warming. Red areas show the most warming.

The ice sheets are difficult to study because they are located in remote and harsh environments. One way scientists study them is by using satellites.

From their locations in space, satellites can measure the heights all across the ice sheets. If the heights are increasing, the ice is getting thicker. If the heights are decreasing, the ice is growing thinner.

Aura, a NASA satellite, studies air quality and the composition of Earth's atmosphere.

In 2010 an enormous chunk of ice, roughly 97 square miles (251 square kilometers) in size, broke off the coast of Greenland.

MASSIVE MELTDOWN

Scientists estimate that the melting Greenland ice sheet is losing about 110 million Olympic size swimming pools worth of water every year.

Scientists collect data to understand how Greenland's glaciers are changing.

Scientists also travel to Greenland and Antarctica to measure conditions of the ice sheets. They place suitcase-sized measuring devices on the ice. These devices measure temperature, air pressure, and wind speed. The data is **transmitted** via satellites so researchers can track the melting closely.

Scientists collect many measurements from different parts of the ice over many years. With these measurements they can learn how much water is going into the ocean. They can then predict how much and how fast the oceans will rise.

To understand Earth's melting ice, scientists travel to remote locations and work in extreme conditions.

CHAPTER FOUR

SHIFTING SEASONS

As Earth's climate warms, the seasons are shifting. Spring is showing up earlier around the world. Fall is happening later. Scientists want to learn how plants and animals are responding to these shifts.

Plants and animals take their cues from the changing seasons. Scientists want to know, are flowers blooming earlier? Are birds shifting when they **migrate** or where they live?

Water samples from a lake can reveal how conditions in the lake are changing.

Different places around the world respond differently to climate change. For example, the Arctic is warming much faster than other places. Because there are so many places for scientists to monitor, they need help. They get help from volunteers, called citizen scientists.

Citizen scientists observe and record seasonal changes in their backyards and neighborhoods. All over the world, they collect data on natural events, such as the timing of flowering or where birds live.

ACTIVITY

NATURE JOURNAL

Grab a piece of paper and a pen or pencil. Find a place to sit outside, or sit inside at a window. Draw what you see going on outdoors. You might draw a cloud, a tree, a flower, or a bird flying by. Then describe what you see in writing.

Careful observations by citizen scientists help fill in details about what is happening all over the world. These details reveal how plants and animals are responding to climate change. Scientists then use this information to study the changes that are taking place and how living things are affected.

By collecting insect specimens, scientists can study how living things are responding to warmer conditions.

EARLY FLOWERS

The blooming of cherry trees in Washington, D.C., is a sign of spring. But as the climate grows warmer, the cherry trees are blooming earlier. One study showed that the blooming of the cherry trees moved earlier by seven days from 1970 to 1999.

Scientists want to learn how plants respond to rising temperatures and carbon dioxide levels.

In the past, gardeners and naturalists took notes about plants, animals, and the timing of natural events. These journals and diaries give us clues about the recent past. Scientists can compare the data from a hundred years ago with new data to see patterns in how living things are being affected by climate change.

CHAPTER FIVE

CLUES FROM MUD AND ICE

When climate scientists want to learn about climate from the distant past, they can look for clues buried in the Earth. Climate always leaves a trace, similar to the way a passing animal can leave its tracks in the mud. By reading the clues, scientists can understand how Earth's climate has changed over time.

Layered rock formation at Valley of Fire State Park, near Las Vegas, Nevada.

Drilled from ice sheets, ice cores contain layer after layer of snow that fell, never melted, and turned to ice.

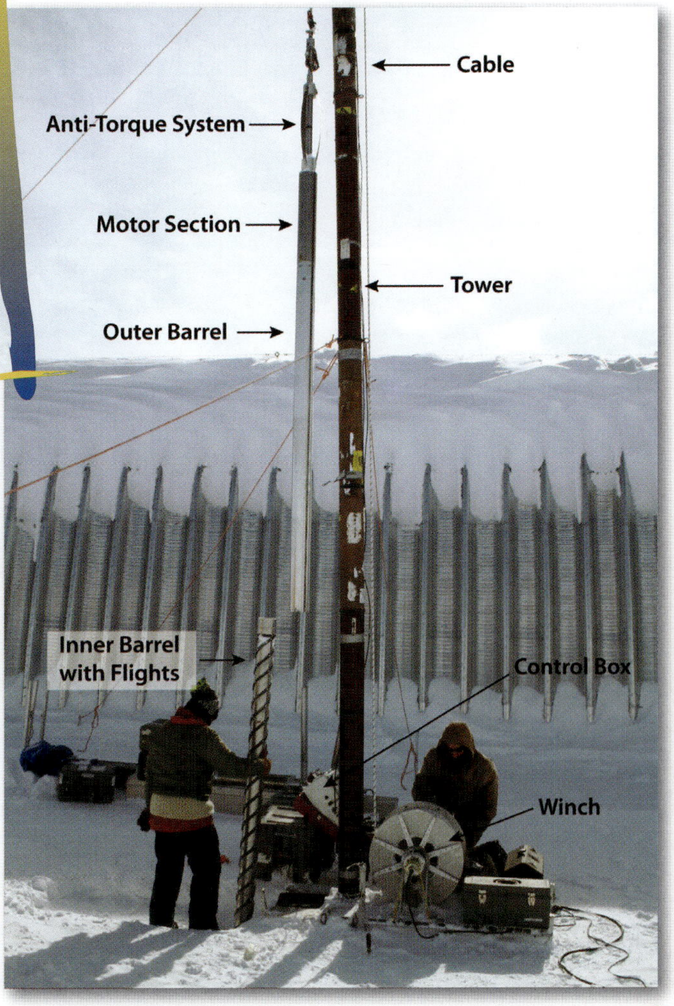

In Greenland and Antarctica, scientists drill ice cores from the ice sheets. Snow falls year-round in both places. Summer snow and winter snow show up as distinct layers. Over many years, the layers of snow turn to ice.

By looking at the layers in ice cores, scientists can see a record of year-to-year changes. For example, the thickness of a layer reveals how much snow fell in that year.

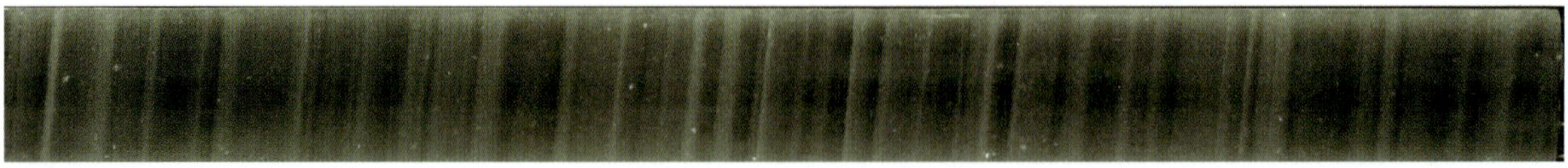

Annual changes in weather show up in ice cores, with summer layers sandwiched between winter layers.

ICY DRILLING

Ice cores from the poles can be several miles long. Researchers cut them into lengths of 3.2 feet (one meter) to make them easier to handle.

Bubbles of air trapped in the ice tell the makeup of the ancient atmosphere. These same bubbles provide chemical clues that reveal past temperatures. Ash, pollen, and dust trapped in the ice can give more clues about the ancient climate and events around the globe.

Gas bubbles trapped in ice help scientists learn about past temperatures.

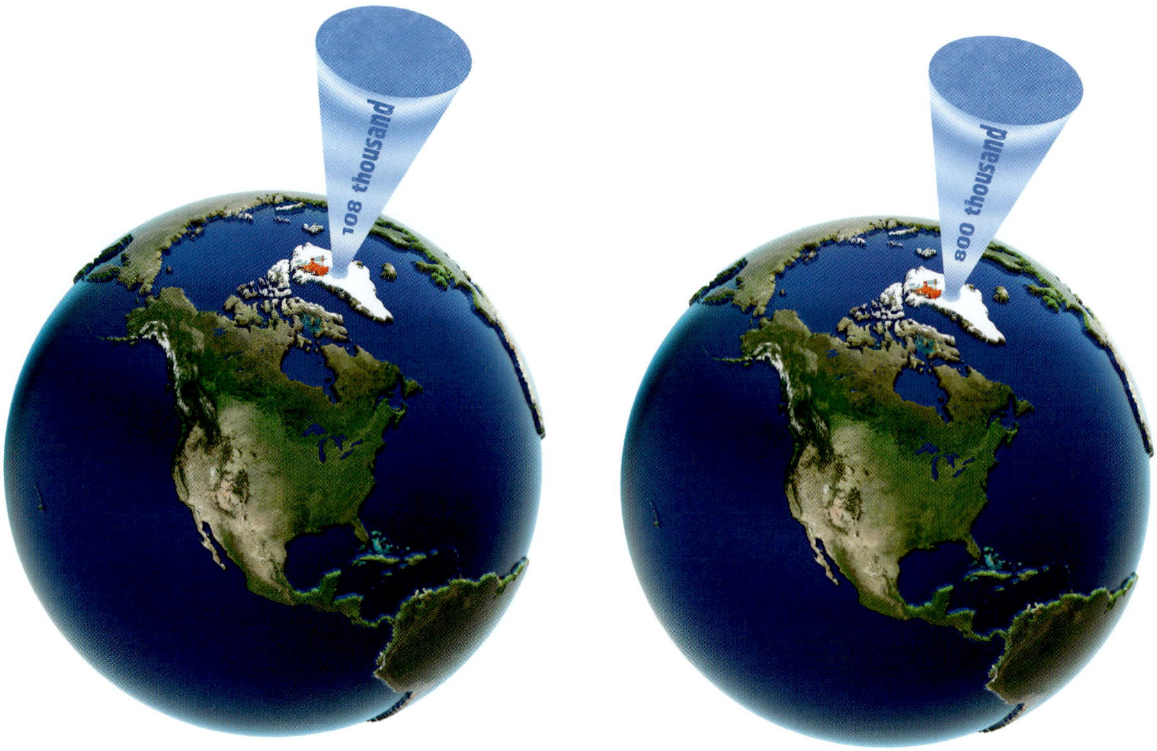

The ice sheet in Greenland gives a record of the climate that stretches back 108,000 years. The record on Antarctica goes back even further to 800,000 years.

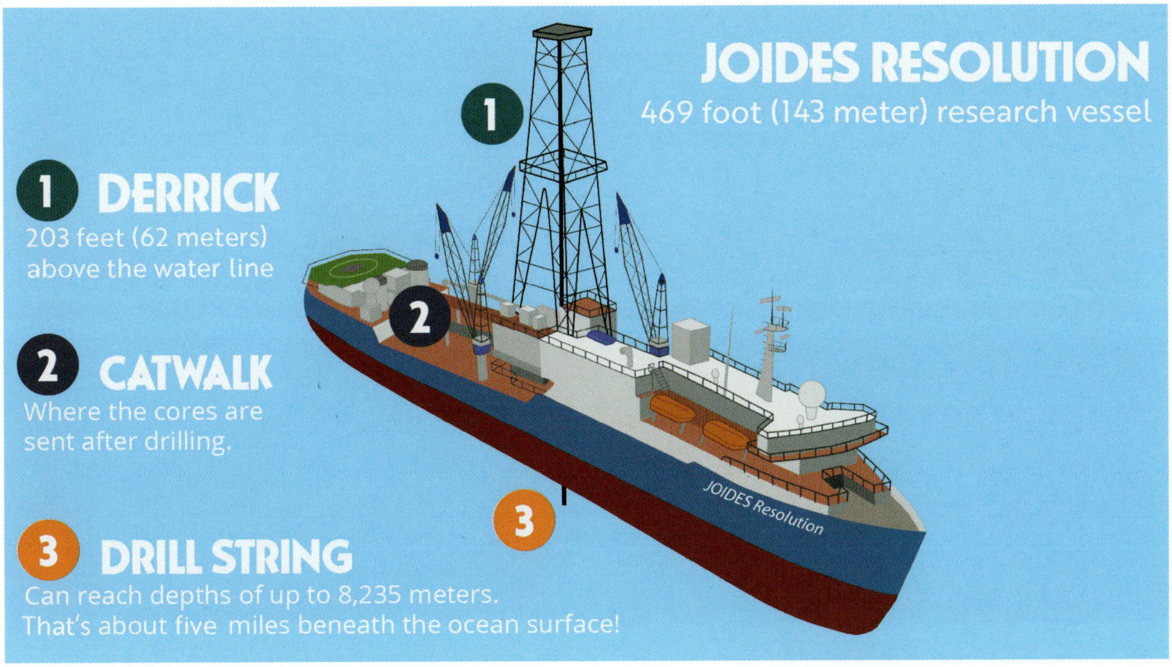

If scientists want to look back even further in turn, they can drill into the sea floor. Ocean **sediment** continually rains down on the sea floor. This sediment forms a layer up to 5.6 miles (9 kilometers) thick. It contains a record stretching back 200 million years.

The Resolution uses pipes and drills to take sediment cores (inset) from the ocean floor.

The ocean floor receives a steady rain of dust, plants, and animal skeletons that settle in layers.

Most ocean sediment is made of tiny shells of **microscopic** sea life. Because different types of sea life survive in different ocean conditions, these fossils are a way to study what the ancient ocean was like.

For example, large amounts of one type of fossil could reveal that those waters were once icy cold.

A RECORD IN RINGS

Tree rings can give important clues about past climates. Each ring is a record of one year of growth. The rings can reveal droughts or fires that occurred during the tree's lifetime.

As with ice cores, ocean sediment can contain pollen, ash, and dust. These **particles** give more clues to past conditions and events around the world.

Wind-swept desert sands can land on the ocean's surface and eventually settle on the ocean floor.

MUDDY WATERS

When dust from desert windstorms shows up in ocean sediment, scientists can learn how dry and dusty the climate may have been. Chemical tests can reveal where the dust came from. This can indicate where the winds were blowing and how strong they were.

CHAPTER SIX

THE FUTURE CLIMATE

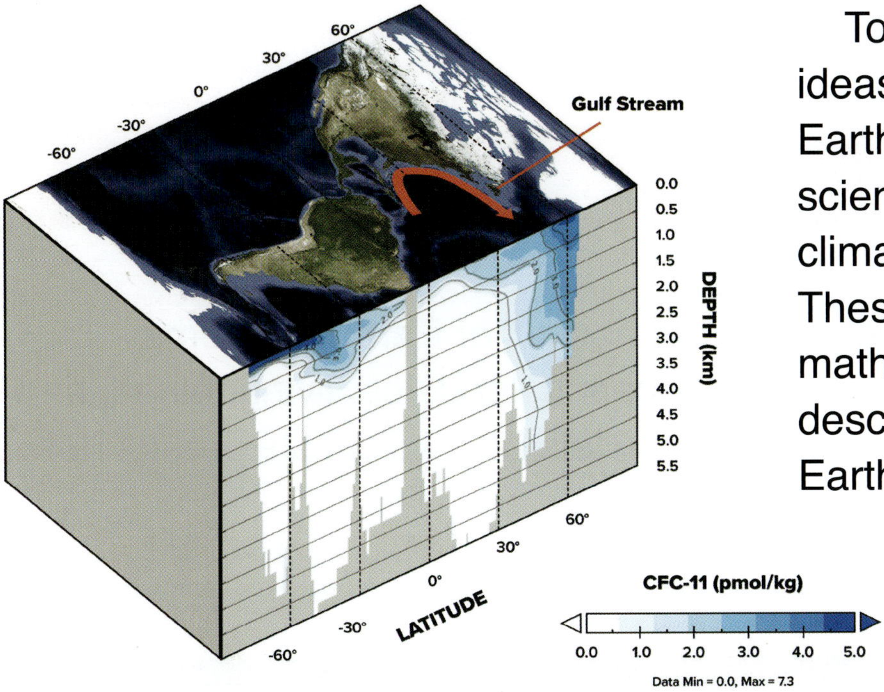

To test their ideas about Earth's climate, scientists build climate models. These models use math problems to describe how the Earth works.

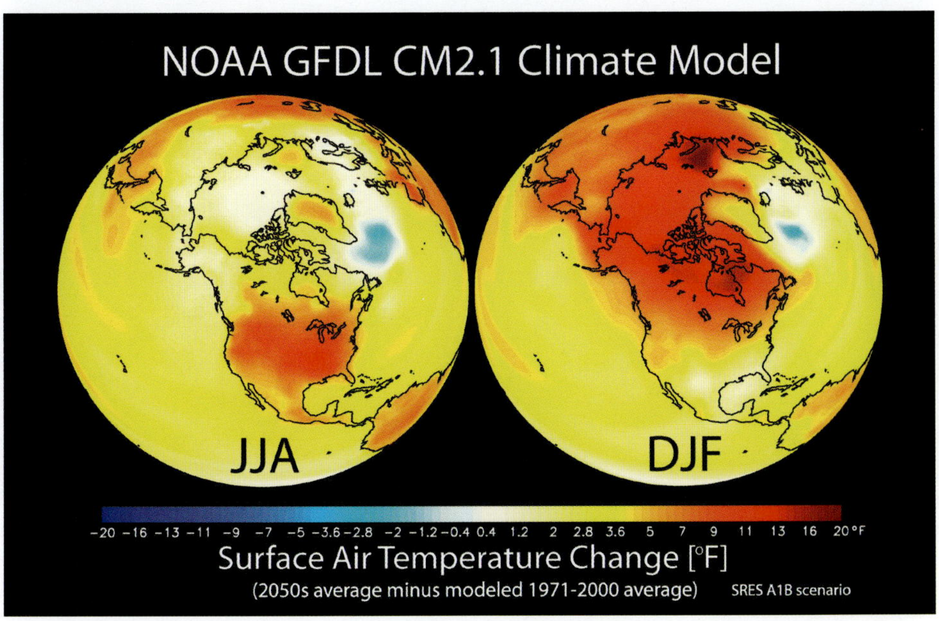

MATH WHIZ

Some climate models contain so many math problems that they must be run on the fastest supercomputers. These supercomputers can perform more than 80 million math problems in an hour.

Climate models consider how all of Earth's systems interact: the atmosphere, oceans, land, ice, living things, and energy from the sun. The models help scientists predict how the climate will change in the future.

Climate models take into account various Earth systems such as global winds and wind patterns that cover long distances.

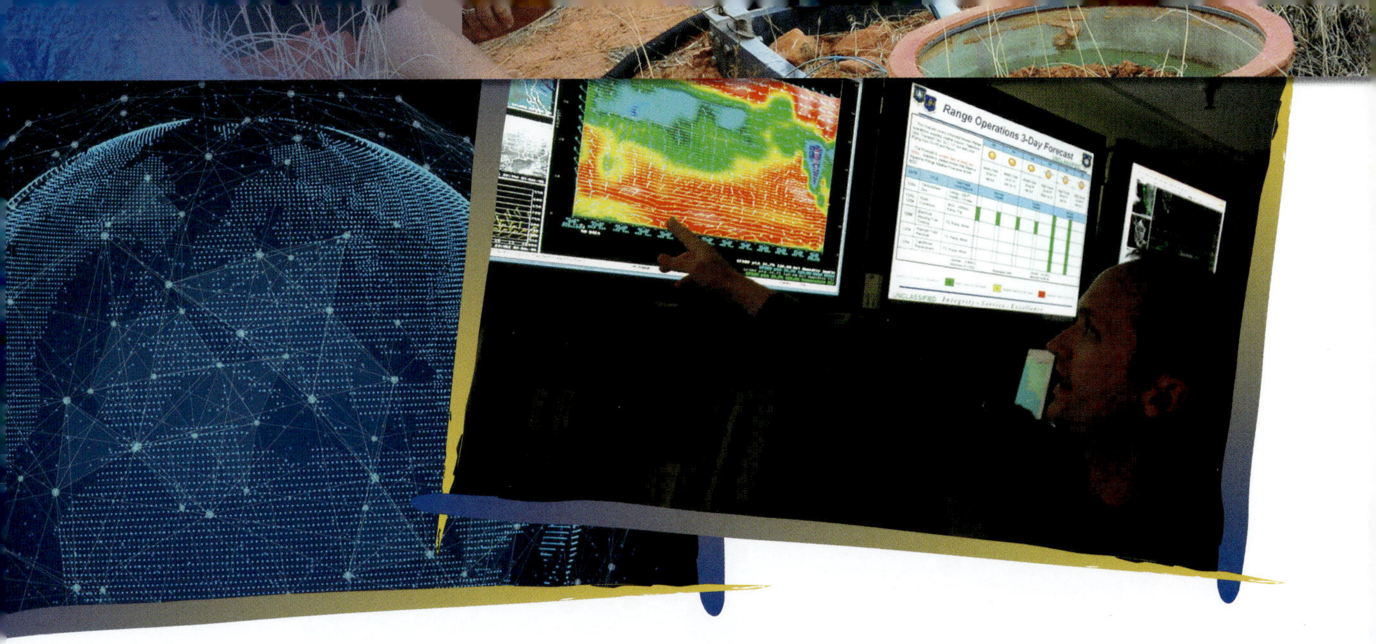

Climate models use an imaginary three-dimensional grid to cover the surface of the Earth. The grid isn't real. It is part of the model. The model runs math problems for every point on the grid.

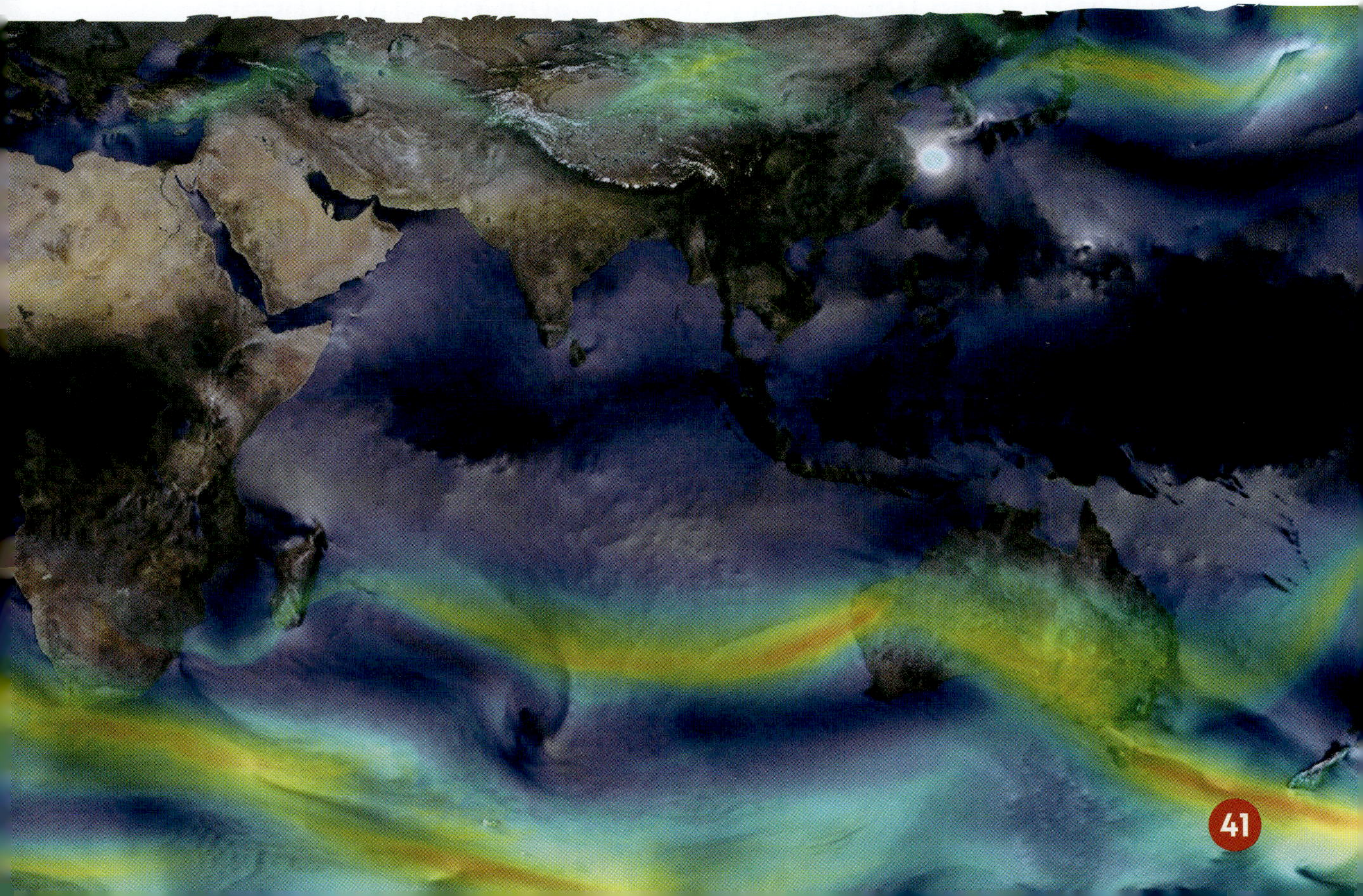

Some models have a grid with wide spacings. There are fewer points for the model to calculate. These models run fast but give less detail.

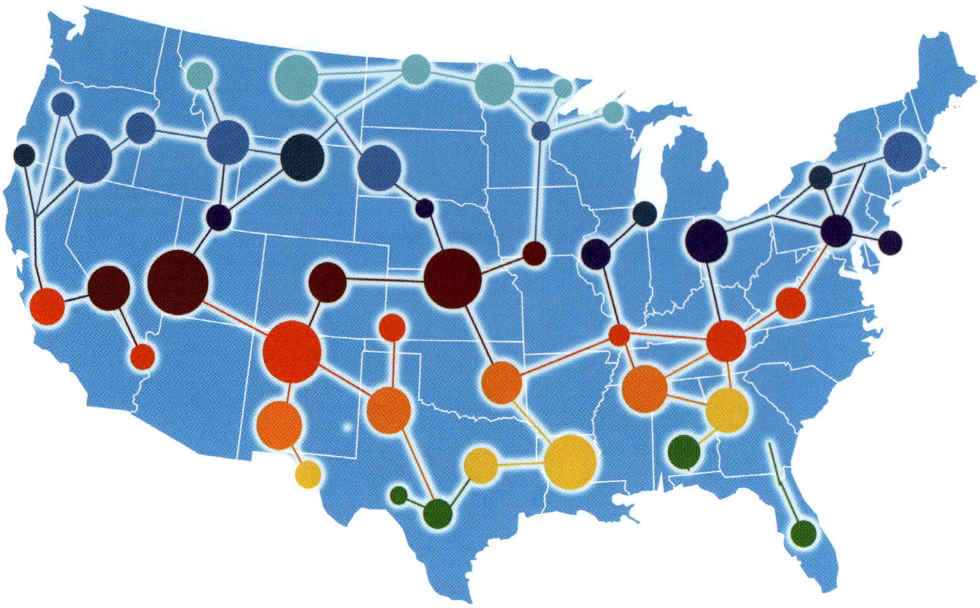

Some models use a very closely spaced grid. These models give more detail but can take a long time for the fastest supercomputer to run.

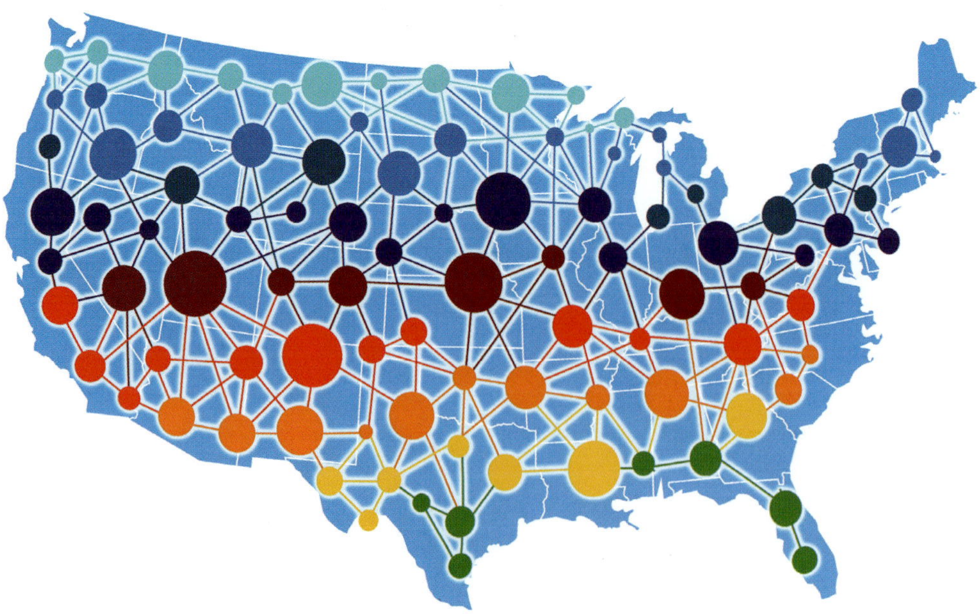

EARTH SIMULATOR

The National Center for Atmospheric Research runs a complex model of the Earth's climate system. This model uses about three trillion math calculations to ***simulate*** *one day on Earth.*

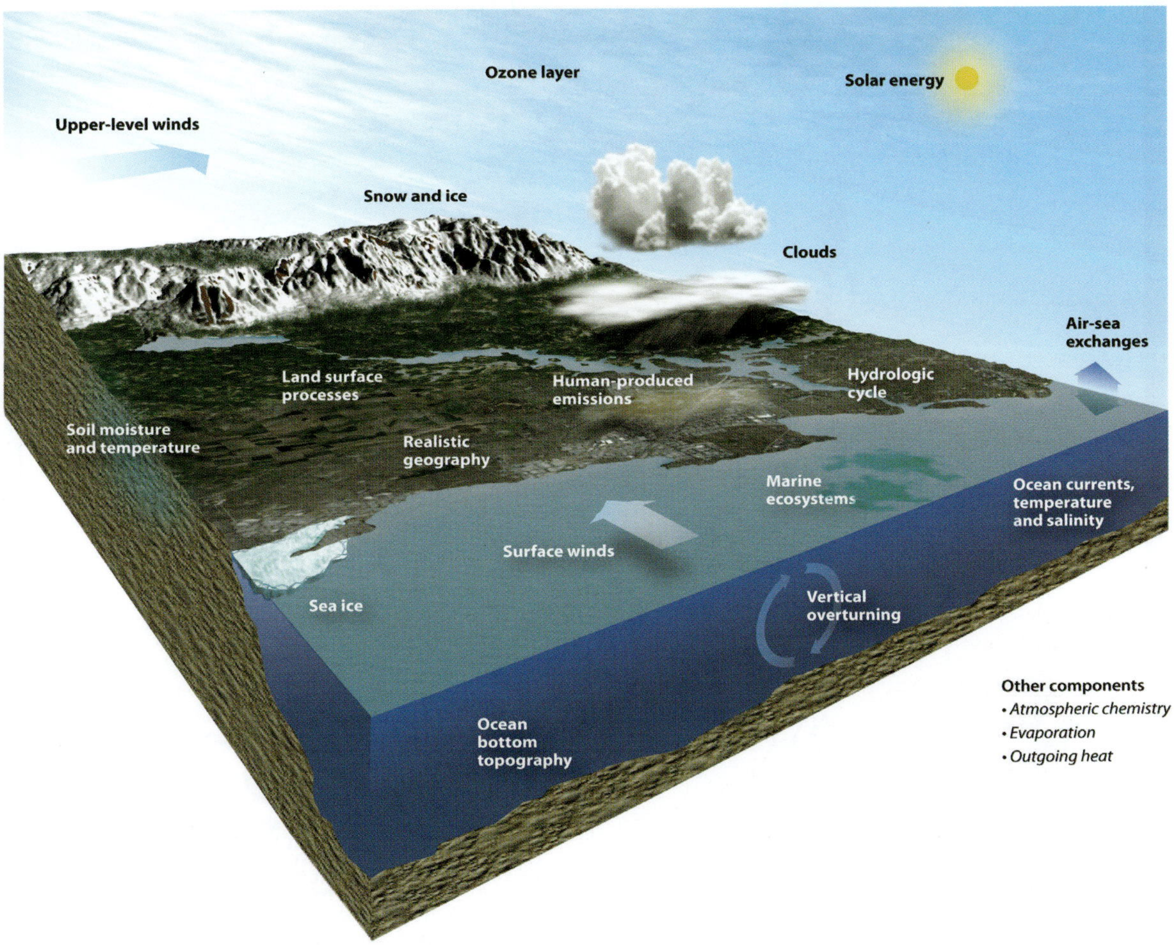

To know whether their climate models are accurate, scientists give their models real-world tests. If a model can simulate what really happened, then scientists have more confidence that the model can accurately predict the future.

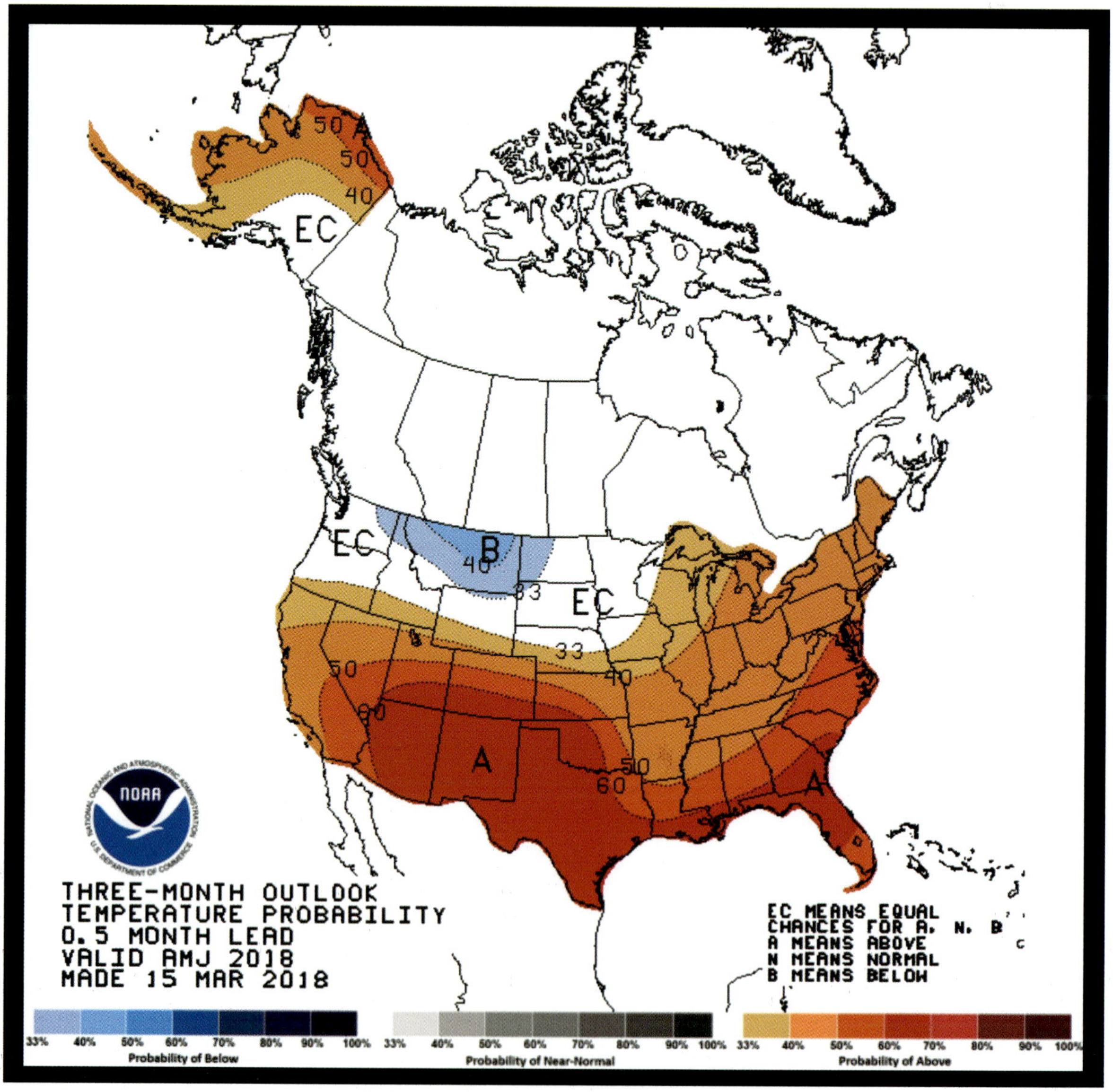

With climate models, scientists can predict the risk of hurricanes and other damaging storms.

Scientists use climate models to look hundreds of years into the future and try to predict what will happen to our climate. They can make predictions about temperature, rainfall, and the probability of extreme weather events.

So what's in store? Climate models predict that Earth's average temperature will continue to rise over the next hundred years. Around the world, scientists will be at work trying to understand these changes.

Glossary

absorb (ab-ZORB): to take in from the air

atmosphere (AT-muh-sfeer): the mass of air surrounding the Earth that contains a mix of nitrogen, oxygen, carbon dioxide, and other gases

glaciers (GLAY-shurs): slow-moving masses of ice found in mountain valleys or polar regions

microscopic (meye-kruh-SKAHP-ik): so small to be visible only with a microscope

migrate (MEYE-grate): to move from one place to another on a regular schedule with the seasons

observatory (uhb-ZUHRV-uh-tor-ee): a place equipped with instruments for observing and measuring natural events

particles (PAHR-ti-kuhls): very small pieces of matter

sediment (SED-uh-muhnt): material in a liquid that settles to the bottom

simulate (SIM-yoo-late): to produce a computer model of something

transmitted (tranz-MIT-ed): sent a signal from a satellite in space to Earth

Index

Show What You Know

1. What can ice cores tell us about past climates?
2. How could you learn what the climate was like two hundred years ago in your city or town?
3. What can satellites reveal about the Greenland ice sheet? Explain three ways climate change affects human health.
4. What animals might be affected by shifting seasons where you live?
5. How do scientists test whether their climate models are accurate?

Further Reading

Herman, Gail, *What Is Climate Change?*, Penguin Workshop, 2018.

Sneideman, Joshua, *Climate Change: Discover How It Impacts Spaceship Earth*, Nomad, 2015.

Basher, Simon, *Basher Science: Climate Change*, Kingfisher, 2016.

About the Author

Rebecca E. Hirsch, Ph.D., earned her doctorate in molecular biology from the University of Wisconsin. She lives in Pennsylvania with her husband and children. She is the author of more than sixty books about science and discovery for children and teens. You can visit her online at www.rebeccahirsch.com.

www.rourkeeducationalmedia.com

PHOTO CREDITS: Credits: istock.com, shutterstock.com. Cover images courtesy of USGS; Pg4; Dreamframer, SteveAllenPhoto. Pg05; JM_Image_Factory, Tomwang112 Pg06; TheCrimsonRibbon, NASA. Pg07; NASA, Pg08; theconsensusproject.com, NASA,Geribody. Pg09; Milena Moiola. Pg10; gorodenkoff, Tenedos Pg11; Antrey, AdrianHancu. Pg12; johannes86, carcar797. Pg13; NOAA, saildrone. com, Pg14; NASA; Pg15; traveler1116, NOAA, Major General Adolphus Washington Greely, head of the weather service, 1887-1891; Pg16; NOAA, NASA. Pg17; Serjio74, Ridofranz. pg 18; Ana Iacob, NOAA, consulgian. Pg19; JohnCarnemolla, NASA. Pg20; NASA/GSFC Scientific Visualization Studio, NASA. Pg22; Capricorn4049 (CCA-4.0 International), Pg23; Joel Harper, University of Montana, GlacierNPS (CCA-2.0). Pg24; USO, Gary Gray. Pg25; BrianEKushner, standret. Pg26; EvgeniyShkolenko, Pg27; Rawpixel, lamyai, HEMARAT. Pg28; Christian Arthur, BackyardProduction, Pg29; Wavebreakmedia, NicoElNino. Pg30; raphoto, Krugloff. Pg31; www.nsf.gov, icecores. org/USGS. Pg32; USGS, National Snow and Ice Data Center Pg33; Atmospheric Research, CSIRO CCA-3.0, NOAA. Pg34; 1xpert, tarras79, National Snow and Ice Data Center. Pg35; Arito Sakaguchi & IODP/TAMU - http://iodp.tamu.edu/publicinfo/copyright.html, Hannes Grobe (talk)-CCA3.0. Pg36; Pg37; y-studio, Matauw. Pg38; donvictorio, Gabriele Maltinti. Pg39; NOAA, Pg40; NOAA PG41; Mirexon. PG42;shoo_arts, RosLilly, PG43; ©UCAR. GenGen -CCA-2.1_Japan. Pg44; gorodenkoff Pg45; Petrovich9, Harvepino

Edited by: Keli Sipperley

Produced by Blue Door Education for Rourke Educational Media. Cover and Interior design by: Jennifer Dydyk

Climate Scientists at Work / Rebecca E. Hirsch
(Taking Earth's Temperature)
ISBN 978-1-64156-452-6 (hard cover)
ISBN 978-1-64156-578-3 (soft cover)
ISBN 978-1-64156-696-4 (e-Book)
Library of Congress Control Number: 2018930479

Rourke Educational Media
Printed in the United States of America, North Mankato, Minnesota